Barhopping into History

London, Ontario

by:
Kym Wolfe (Author)
&
Cheryl Radford (Artist)

Disclaimer

The factual information included in this book was gleaned from what we believe are credible sources. We have made every effort to ensure the information was correct at press time.

We have included personal opinions and perceptions, drawn from our own observations and from the many individuals we met and interviewed over the past year. You may not see and experience these establishments in the same way.

The publisher, author and artist do not assume and hereby disclaim any liability to any party for any loss, damage, or disruption caused by errors or omissions, whether such errors or omissions result from negligence, accident, or any other cause.

Additional copies of this book and contact information for the author and artist are available at http://barhoppingintohistory.blogspot.ca

ISBN 978-0-9921356-0-7

Production Credits
    Book Design: Cheryl Radford
    Copy Editing: Amanda Burdick
    Publisher: ChKs Publishing, London, ON

Acknowledgements

So many people have had a hand in bringing this book to life, we can't possibly thank them all by name. We would like to extend our sincere thanks to the bar owners, staff and patrons who generously shared their time and stories; our family and friends who buffered us with their interest and enthusiasm when we felt ours flagging; Amanda Burdick and Cecilia Buy whose eagle eyes helped polish the prose; Tony Paul for his assistance and expertise in turning traditional drawings into print ready artwork; Jacob Wolfe who provided invaluable editorial input; Mike Baker who let us pick his brain and steered us in the right direction; staff at London Public Library who helped locate sources of historical information; and the architects, builders and craftsmen who designed and created these beautiful buildings.

Cheryl Radford acknowledges
the generous support of the

London **Arts** Council

Contents

Cheryl   Kym

Introduction

We created this book to share our love of London's wonderful historic architecture, along with trivia about the city's past. We thought barhopping would give us an interesting link to centre our stories and drawings around, and decided to focus on historic buildings that are now used as bars.

We used 1826, the year London was declared a townsite, as our starting point. When we learned that London's first official business was a tavern, it confirmed for us that the concept of Barhopping into History had been a good choice.

The settlement's first home belonged to Peter McGregor. By some accounts he hung a tin cup on his door jamb; others says he chopped down a tree and set a whiskey bottle on the stump; all agree that the day after London was officially founded, Mr. McGregor declared his "tavern" open for business. You will find a historic plaque at 45 King Street at the corner of Ridout, honouring Mr. McGregor as London's first settler, first innkeeper and first entrepreneur.

To narrow our focus, we set three criteria for the buildings and bars that would be included in the book:

  ◆ buildings are within the boundaries that were in place in 1855, when London officially became a city;

  ◆ buildings are more than 100 years old;

  ◆ buildings are in current use as bars or pubs and viewed primarily as drinking establishments.

Through our research we also came across snippets of London's history that have nothing to do with bars or historic buildings. You'll find some of them sprinkled throughout the book.

We hope you enjoy this selective glimpse into some of London's historic buildings and the bars that occupy them today.

Cheers!
Kym and Cheryl

Barhopping Locations of London

ADELAIDE ST.

COLBORNE ST.

SOUTH ST.

NELSON ST.

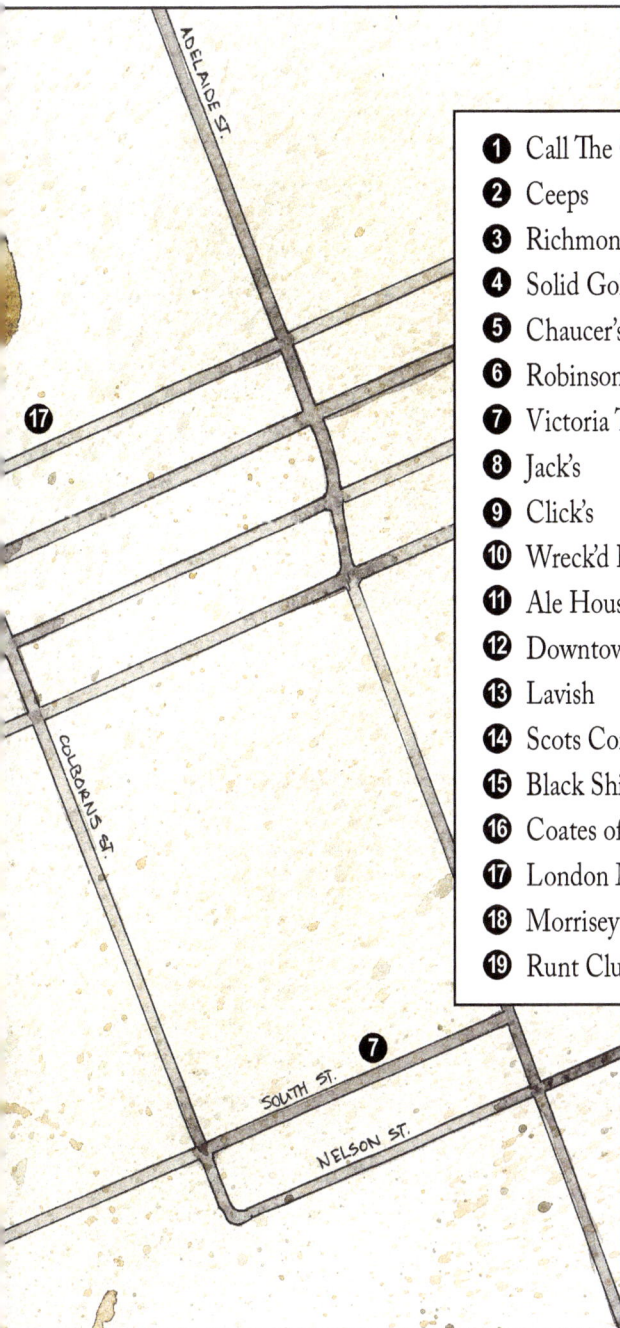

❶ Call The Office
❷ Ceeps
❸ Richmond Tavern
❹ Solid Gold
❺ Chaucer's
❻ Robinson Hall
❼ Victoria Tavern
❽ Jack's
❾ Click's
❿ Wreck'd Room
⓫ Ale House
⓬ Downtown Kathy Brown's
⓭ Lavish
⓮ Scots Corner
⓯ Black Shire
⓰ Coates of Arms
⓱ London Music Club
⓲ Morrisey House
⓳ Runt Club

⓱

❼

The Original Taverns of London

Peter McGregor opened London's first tavern in 1826 at the corner of King and Ridout streets. His establishment is long gone, but four hotel taverns that opened in the 1800s are still standing and operating as bars today.

When they first opened, the upstairs rooms were rented to travelers and were also permanent addresses of many working class Londoners. The main floors served as gathering places where people could have a drink and a meal, talk business, catch up on the news and enjoy the camaraderie of their peers.

In many ways hotel taverns were the community centres of their time. They were sometimes used for public meetings, as a place for travelling salesmen to show their products, to stage political events or for other like purposes.

In time a cluster of high-end hotels would open near the financial district, the courthouse and the forks of the Thames. Canada's first oil wells were drilled in 1858 in Oil Springs, just west of London; in the mid-1860s a local businessman tapping for oil at the forks of the Thames hit the sulphur springs instead. The Sulphur Springs and Mineral Bath spa propelled London to fame as a health resort and attracted visitors from across North America.

The Ontario Temperance Act, enacted in 1916 as a war measure, decimated the hotel tavern industry. Only 17 of London's 170 drinking establishments survived, relying on room rentals and non-alcoholic hospitality sales to keep their doors open. There may well have been some private drinking going on; although it was illegal to sell alcohol in public places, distilleries and breweries could still legally produce it.

Fun Facts:

Regulars at *Call The Office* will tell you they have either seen or felt the presence of a ghost – a woman who some believe was murdered here. Others say that she didn't die here, but was murdered in her home; afterwards her killer came directly to the tavern for a good stiff drink.

The *Ceeps* is the only historic pub in the city with a brew house on site. Ceeps Ale is brewed year-round; one-off batches of seasonal fruit beers are available for summer sipping on Barney's patio, London's largest downtown patio bar.

The *Richmond Tavern*, London's oldest continually operating hotel and historic tavern, was rumoured to be a hotbed for spies during the American civil war.

John J. O'Flaherty, long-time hotel proprietor at what is currently *Solid Gold*, was well known at race tracks across the continent. His stable of horses competed on all principal U.S. and Canadian tracks in the early 1900s.

CALL THE OFFICE

The Jon Spencer Blues Explosion. THE SELECTER. Sebadoh
BLOODSHOT BILL. SO YOUNG. The Bicycles. The Abbreviations
Indie Underground. HOLLERADO. PUP. Slim Cessna's Auto Club
KEN MODE. The Standstills. FULL OF HELL. BY DIVINE RIGHT. catl
The BIGSOUND minitour. Halfway to Barstow. Pie in the Sky Captain
Bringdown. PLAN 37. Child Bite. Electric Six. Barnburner
SONNY Vincent. MONESARAM. Matt Mays. The Zellots. FLATLINER
The Ketamines. MADBALL. Say Domino. Don't Touch The Dancers
Mad Caddies. THE CREEPSHOW. Fucked Up. Moon King. S.H.I.T.
HELLBOUND HEPCATS. The Hounds Below. Great Bloomers
Hillbilly Bugger Boys. le Guttermouth. PHANTOGRAM. Tim Barry
Old Man Markley. BLACK N BLUEGRASS. Hostage Life. Sick of it All
Zeus. UBT. Northern Pikes. Crash Test Dummies. TEENAGE HEAD
Queens of the Stone Age. OUR LADY PEACE. The New Outcasts
More More. Skeletons. LOW. blink 182. Tea Party. The Arketts
Danko Jones. rimson

CALL THE OFFICE
BAR & NIGHT CLUB

CALL THE OFFICE
THURSDAY
FUNTAK
SUNDAY
RATGUN

Call The Office ❶

216 York Street

The first recorded occupant at this address (Atlantic House hotel and stable yard) appears in the City Directory in 1881. Since then it has been the Salvation Army Military Hostel, Salvation Army Home for Girls, the Hotel Bodega, the York Hotel and, since 1984, Call The Office.

In the 1960s and '70s the bar was an informal clubhouse for local artists and intellectuals. It was described as having an underground, Bohemian feel. It made its mark as a live music mecca, with a different band every night playing mainly bluegrass, jazz and rhythm and blues.

A newspaper clipping from 1970 describes it this way: "The York for some strange reason runs the whole gamut from the mailman who pops in for a beer after work to the professional who drops in for entertainment in the evenings to the swinging, younger generation who like their music loud and long."

The Nihilist Spasm Band was born here and played the York pretty much every Monday night into the 1970s. This eclectic group of local artists, professionals and retirees, playing kazoos and various home-made and mismatched instruments, represented Canada in 1969 as our official music team at the Sixth Biennale des Jeunes in Paris, France.

Today Call The Office continues to be a hotbed for original music, attracting talent from around the globe. Artists have come from across North America and Europe, and some from as far away as Australia and Japan, to play in this iconic bar. A roster of past musicians can be seen in posters that paper the brick walls and cover the spectrum from rock, punk, and blues to modern indie music.

Although the bar is fully stocked, a sign bearing a massive Labatt 50 beer bottle hangs over one end of the bar and is a testament to the manager's claim that, above all, "50 rules!"

CPR
TAVERN
&
BREW PUB

Barney's

SLEDGE HAMMER
BINGO

your GRANDFATHER drank here
your FATHER drank here
your SON someday
will too!

The Ceeps ❷

This hotel opened in 1890 as the Grand Pacific. In 1907 it became the CPR Hotel, named either for the Canadian Pacific Railway or for Comfort, Peace and Rest. In the mid-1950s the hotel's Bamboo Room cocktail lounge and Starlite Dining Room were popular London night spots because there were no other licensed establishments along that stretch of Richmond Street.

Since 1991 the Ceeps has been brewing its own house draft, and is the only historic bar in the city with its own micro-brew operation. If you sit in the right spot in the bar you can see the brewer in action.

The tavern has been an iconic part of the Western experience since the 1800s. It was Western students who shortened the name to the Ceeps in the 1960s. During the annual fall homecoming weekend the university's alumni are inevitably drawn back to their old hangout, which now includes Barney's. Named in memory of long-time bartender Barney Hughes, Barney's has London's largest downtown patio bar.

The Ceeps has sealed its place in students' hearts in part because the owners have adapted as students have changed, offering activities like Sledgehammer Bingo (introduced in 2005) and the now defunct beach volleyball on Barney's patio. Winners of the weekly Sledgehammer Bingo games get to don a plastic poncho and take a sledgehammer to a variety of fruit. Along with bragging rights, winners walk away with prizes, usually adult themed toys and novelty items.

In the 1980s hundreds of students left their mark by carving the tops of the bar's large round wooden tables. Only three of those round tables have survived. Two are fairly easy to spot, but to find the third one you'll have to look up….it's hiding in plain sight in the new Bamboo Room.

The RICHMOND TAVERN est 1852

DOMESTIC BOTTLES

Matinee EVERY WEEK

Enjoy LIVE MUSIC

Pitchers (ICE-COLD)

10

The Richmond Tavern ❸
372 Richmond Street at King

Built in 1852 by grocer D.W.C. Day, and converted to Arkell's Hotel in 1860, the Richmond has the distinction of being the oldest surviving hotel tavern in the city.

During the American Civil War (1861-65) it operated as the Revere House Hotel. Agents from both sides of the U.S. conflict used the hotel as their headquarters when they came across the border to purchase supplies, and it had the reputation of being a hotbed for spies.

Renamed the Richmond in 1893, it has long been known as a neighbourhood working-class bar. The bar stocks wine, spirits and bottled beer, but close to 85% of what goes over the counter is in a draft glass.

Years ago it was a networking haven where work crews would come for a cold one before heading home. An unemployed person looking for a temporary gig could make a few connections and leave with a job lined up for the next day.

The regulars here are like extended family. They banter back and forth, celebrate the milestones and mourn the deaths. On one table a plaque honours 'Marie Morton, Queen of the Richmond since 1918', a woman who came for a daily draft for more than 40 years. A wall plaque proclaims the Richmond as 'Kirby's Head Office' with the poignant message, "You're sadly missed with your laughter...Rest in Peace."

By 10 or 11 p.m. younger patrons fill the bar. They enjoy live music Thursday, Friday and Saturday nights - heavy metal, punk or rock, and occasionally country or bluegrass. Sunday is karaoke night.

For the most part, the Richmond is simply a quiet place in the heart of downtown where people come to have a drink, play some pool, share a few stories or simply watch the world go by.

Solid GOLD

NON STOP ACTION
4PM TO 2AM

The building that Solid Gold occupies started its life in 1876 as the Victoria House Hotel, but it may best be remembered for the many years it spent as the Savoy Hotel.

With its curved windows topped by ornamental detailing and stylish awnings, the hotel was an attractive building. It was occupied by both short-term travelers and longer-term roomers and, like many older hotels, it is rumoured to have its resident ghosts.

If you look at the building today, you will see two archways at street level. One is the entrance to the bar. The other was originally an open access that is now walled off. It went through the building, allowing travelers to ride into a courtyard where a livery stable was located behind the hotel.

A variety of bars operated on the main floor before Solid Gold opened in 1986. Today the regulars would argue that the most attractive part of the bar can be found inside, where a bevy of beauties perform on stage every night. As the oldest and only surviving strip club in the core area, Solid Gold holds a unique place in London's history.

The bar bills itself as "London's finest gentlemen's club." However the staff and dancers tell us they have noticed a shift with younger patrons. They often see young heterosexual couples come in together to watch the dancers. Still, on any given night you are apt to find more men than women here.

The men tell us it's not just about the beautiful women, it's also about the camaraderie. And it's an interesting place to people watch while you are hanging out and having a drink with the guys.

Old and Interesting

Chaucer's is not quite a century building, but it is an extension of the Marienbad, which was built in 1854. An early tenant was the London Free Press, which began operating here as a daily newspaper in 1855. This was also the site of the Queen's Hotel, one of London's finest establishments and known for its elegant dining room.

Robinson Hall's architecture is unique among core area bars, and a testament to the money that was poured into stately financial institutions to ensure they appeared prosperous. Banks were a critical part of London's early commercial growth. The Bank of Upper Canada (435 Ridout Street) was built in 1835 and is likely one of the oldest bank structures in Canada.

Robinson Hall also stands in a historically significant location, beside Covent Garden Market and near the stretch of King Street that was once known as Whiskey Row. The earliest market operated in this area in 1835. Eventually a block of taverns and hotels sprang up across from it on King Street. The notorious strip, Whiskey Row, was known for its many fights and occasional murders, and women would only walk there if they had an escort.

The *Victoria Tavern,* a venerable bar in London's history, closed just before we went to print. It was a long-term neighbourhood gathering place, uniquely located outside of the city centre but within London's original city boundaries.

Fun Facts:

The chimney sweep is a sign of good luck in Great Britain and central Europe. The nearly six foot metal figure perched on *Chaucer's* roof has been there since the pub opened in 1975.

Bank buildings like *Robinson Hall* were established mainly to extend credit to merchants, and as savings and loans operations for local business owners. Banks were not allowed to offer mortgages until 1967.

Both the *Victoria Tavern* and Victoria Hospital, which opened in 1899, were named for Britain's longest serving monarch. Queen Victoria reigned for 63 years, 7 months and 2 days before her death in 1901.

Good
luck
omen

Chaucer's ❺

122 Carling Street

This address was the original location of the London Free Press, built by Josiah Blackburn in 1854. It later housed the Queen's Hotel. The Farmer's Advocate, Canada's longest published agricultural journal with a 99-year run, had its offices here from 1920 until it closed in 1965.

An extension to the orginal building was added around 1925. Fifty years and many businesses later, it became Chaucer's. The sidewalk patio and the nearly six foot tall chimney sweep on the roof have been here since the pub opened.

It is named for Geoffrey Chaucer, the English poet from the Middle Ages. In deference to the building's literary and publishing roots, there are large letters mounted behind the bar – pieces of type that came from a functioning printing press.

Chaucer's has the cozy feel of a European pub, with wood decor, a fireplace and a collection of interesting items, including a clock from London's original railway station that still keeps perfect time. The wall paneling, bar and pillars are made from wood that was salvaged from London's old courthouse when the new court was built in 1974.

Beer on tap is a staple in any authentic pub, and the manager tells us Chaucer's had the first Belgian draft tower in Canada.

In the 1980s CBC radio aired live jazz shows from the pub and there is still live music on occasion.

But mostly this is a "thinking person's pub," a little hidden spot of Europe that attracts a broad cross-section of Londoners.

Regulars include lawyers and theatre-goers, ladies who lunch, couples enjoying after dinner drinks and dessert, and students working on a cold one along with their latest assignments.

THORNY DEVIL LOUNGE

ROBINSON HALL BAR & GRILL

Robinson Hall ⑥

Robinson Hall is named after a hotel that was built in 1830 at the corner of Dundas and Ridout Streets. The Great Fire of London (1845) started in Robinson Hall's stables. The hotel was rebuilt and reopened in 1849, but torn down in 1930.

Its namesake, the new Robinson Hall, is a little more than a block away in the historic market area. The elegant Beaux-Arts building dates back to 1912 when it opened as the Bank of British North America; it later became the Bank of Montreal.

Echoes of well-mannered bankers seem to linger in the newest incarnation of Robinson Hall. The stately building has been transformed, with wrought iron detailing, dark wood molding, distinctive artwork and chandeliers that hang over the banquette seating. The former bank vault is now a private drinks area.

The atmosphere at both Robinson Hall (main floor) and Thorny Devil (second floor) is indulgent, reminiscent of the roaring twenties. A tribute to that era can be found in the ladies' room upstairs: a painting of two women dressed for a night on the town with quotes by Dorothy Parker, a writer and critic known for her sharp wit.

Wherever you sit, look down at the tabletop and you'll find a picture, quote, piece of trivia or some other conversation starter – one of owner John Scott-Pearse's personal touches. The table tops and posters upstairs have slogans and pictures with a decidedly more devilish tone than the main floor.

This is a "boy meets girl" kind of bar, with DJs on both floors playing top 40 dance music. The manager tells us the Thorny Devil was the first bar in London, outside of strip clubs, to have poles installed on the dance floor – for use by the ladies only please!

THE VIC

LIVE MUSIC
FRI NIGHT
SUN
WEEKENDS
LICENSED under LCBO

466

*Happy to
share his story!*

Victoria Tavern ❼

466 South Street

This address was a store from the 1920s up until the Victoria Tavern opened in 1933. The pub was named for Britain's longest serving monarch, and you'll still find Queen Victoria's profile on the tavern sign. Inside the atmosphere was always cozier and more casual than the royal name would imply.

From its earliest days you would find a broad mix of people: travelers and lodgers from the rooms upstairs, doctors and staff from Victoria Hospital down the street, workers from nearby factories and people who lived in the neighbourhood.

In some circles the Vic was known as the 'Bucket of Blood'. The nickname goes back to the tavern's early days when bloody brawls would often break out among the hard working - and sometimes hard drinking - clientele.

More recently, people who grew up in the neighbourhood fondly recall Christmas gatherings that were held on December 23 every year. People who had moved away would often come back that night to toast the season, and regulars would step up to sing, play the guitar or the spoons or otherwise contribute to the party.

If you stopped by any afternoon or early evening, you were bound to meet an old-timer with interesting stories to share. Tom, a 71-year-old British chap, told us he was a jockey in his younger days and raced alongside Davey Jones, who later joined The Monkees. "Davey went on to be famous, and I didn't," said Tom wryly, although he was proud to note he did ride in front of crowds that included Winston Churchill, Queen Elizabeth and the Queen Mum.

Tom and other locals would love to sit in the bar again and raise a pint to the Vic. We hold out hope it will reopen and take back its rightful place among London's historic bars.

Repurposed Wholesale

As a critical trade hub, London supplied consumer goods to the surrounding agricultural region. Businessmen made their fortunes importing commodities and food in bulk, packaging them in smaller lots, and reselling them to merchants and general stores across Southwestern Ontario. Warehouses were built to store the goods as they arrived, and many are still part of the downtown streetscape.

The arrival of the railway in 1853 was a game changer. A period map of Western Ontario shows a web of rail lines converging on the city and proclaims that "London as a distributing point is unequalled." Goods could be easily shipped right across the country, and the wholesale district thrived. At one point there were at least ten large wholesale houses within a block of the train station at Richmond and York Streets.

The Waterloo block on Richmond Street (between York and King Streets) was built for the wholesale trade in 1881. The block was designed to impress, with ornamental details and an expensive red brick façade. One of the original occupants was Robinson, Little & Co. dry good wholesalers. Established in 1875, the company was once the largest importer of polished cotton in the British Empire.

Thousands of past Western students can thank partner J.W. Little for providing seating during Mustangs sporting events. Little sat on the University of Western Ontario's original Board of Governors and after his death his family built Western's first stadium in his honour.

The Waterloo block has had its share of bars open and close over the years, but only two low-key but long lasting watering holes remain: Click's and the Wreck'd Room. Above them are remnants of past bars – Club Large, GTs, Burlesque, New Yorker, Ichabods and others – and we have no doubt new ones will open in the future.

539 Richmond Street

Jack's was built circa 1912 by John Dromgole, a wholesaler of china and fancy goods. The tiled floor at the front entry still bears his company name. It was later home to a hat and fur wholesaler, then W.T. Rawleigh Co., a wholesale distributor of medicinal tonics and healthcare products.

Mr. Rawleigh, an 18-year-old from Wisconsin, started selling his products from a horse and buggy in 1889. By 1920 his company had expanded across North America and Australia, opened its own laboratories, and was said to be the largest manufacturer in the world. 'Rawleigh's Good Health Guide Almanac & Cook Book' was printed here in 1921, one of a series of helpful books that the company published.

Today it is Jack's, a bar that bills itself as "London's Party Destination". With a capacity of 1,200 on three floors the bar has a low price/high volume business model that attracts hundreds of students nightly. It has more of a sports bar and pub feel to it earlier in the evening, when people of all ages will drop in for a drink and a bit to eat.

A façade
designed to impress

Click's ⑨

337 Richmond Street (lower level)

One patron summed up Click's this way: "Cheap drinks made well." This is a basic, no frills kind of bar. What draws people in is the comfort of a regular hangout with affordable drinks. You're more likely to find the over 40s here, and the under-40 crowd next door at the Wreck'd Room.

Wreck'd Room ⑩

335 Richmond Street (lower level)

The Wreck'd Room, a play on the concept of "rec room" has a bit of that feel to it. Metallic walls, black lights, a pool table, and comfortable seating – this is a laid back place where people are welcome to dress and dance however they choose.

If there's music playing it will likely be extreme alternative, industrial, EBM or goth. Regulars tell us they're into live role playing games or live action role play, and this is a good place to hang out and meet like-minded people. "It's like a really weird Cheers," says one. "Come here long enough and it's the kind of place where everybody knows your name."

Fun Fact:

As an important wholesale hub, London was once the rail capital of the country. More than 200 trains came and went each day, two-thirds of them carrying goods into and out of the city.

Repurposed Retail

From the mid-1800s, Dundas Street was the go-to destination for London shoppers. In the bustling retail blocks that stretched from Talbot to Wellington Streets grocers, druggists and dry goods stores sold everything from hats to housewares, and more extravagant items like ready-made clothing, jewelry and furs.

Thomas Frazer Kingsmill, an Irish immigrant, opened his dry goods store on Dundas Street in 1865. Today it is the only department store left downtown. Up to the end of 2013 it was still in the family, run by the fifth generation of Kingsmills in the city.

When electricity came to London residences after the turn of the century, the Hydro Shop at the corner of Dundas and Wellington wowed residents with clever marketing events like cooking demonstrations on the new electric range. The Hydro Shop created such a surge in electric appliance sales that, before it closed in 1956, it was credited with Londoners having more electric ranges per capita than any other city in North America.

In the 1950s neon signs lit up the Dundas strip by night. Like bright multi-coloured invitations, they beckoned consumers to visit the movie theatres, restaurants, taverns and the many thriving retailers in the busy city core.

Downtown Kathy Brown's, Lavish, Scots Corner and Ale House are all bars in former retail locations. The Ale House is just east of Wellington; the other three are in the block that runs between Clarence and Wellington Streets. In the 1920s this block was the place to buy a piano, trumpet or other musical instrument, and you will still find music playing here every weekend night.

Each of these four bars has its own style, culture and atmosphere, adding an interesting dash of character to the present-day Dundas streetscape.

Fun Fact:

Retailers have used London as a consumer test market for decades. The city's size, demographic mix and location make it an ideal testing ground for new products and concepts. Experts say if it sells in London, it will sell almost anywhere in Canada.

OPEN THIS LONG WEEKEND
BREAKFAST 10 TO 4
APPS .4PM TO CLOSE
STEAM WHISTLE JUGS
ALL SPORTS ALL DAY

Breakfast Served Daily

Built in 1885, this building was occupied up to 1925 by Catalano & Sansone Fruits. The retailer was affiliated with the Sansone Fruit wholesale company which had its warehouse on Horton Street, and at its peak brought in 14 boxcars of fruit and vegetables daily by rail.

Its neighbour was the Rex Cigar Company, one of almost 20 cigar manufacturers in the city. Rex had the only purpose built cigar factory in London. It is now a bridal shop.

The cigar industry was the city's largest employer. Almost 2,000 workers produced 80 million cigars annually, making London the second largest producer of cigars in the entire country. With WWI and prohibition, demand for cigars dropped significantly; by 1930 only 10 cigar manufacturers remained.

The first restaurant and tavern opened at this address in 1980. The owners planted a tree and grapevines in the open space to the east of the building, and now the mature vines provide shade to the entire patio. The sheltering canopy and the wrought iron gates at the sidewalk create the feel of a European courtyard, tucked away from the noise and traffic of Dundas Street.

The Ale House has been operating here since 2010. The bones of the original building are still evident in the exposed brick walls throughout the pub and the wooden trussed ceiling at the rear of the pub.

The atmosphere is that of a sports and social pub. All of the serving staff wear kilts and bar taps ring the top of the wall. It's a fitting décor theme for a bar that takes pride in its extensive selection of beers and ciders. There are roughly 100 different labels, ranging from standard domestics and imports to craft and premium selections.

Downtown Kathy Brown's

ONTARIO FURNITURE CO.

Downtown Katy Browns

HONEST LAWYER

Downtown Kathy Brown's 12

228 Dundas Street

The first known business at this address was an 1886 grocer that also sold wines and liquors.

That building is long gone, replaced by the Ontario Furniture Company retail store in 1910. Downtown Kathy Brown's has kept the furniture showroom's original wood floor, brick walls and floor-to-ceiling bay windows which provide a panoramic view of Dundas Street lit up at night.

The club is on the building's second floor and is only open Saturday nights. From 9 p.m. until 2 a.m. retro dance music from the 80s and 90s is played live to air on Fresh FM. You'll find all ages on the huge dance floor, although the women far outnumber the men.

In 2013 London was named the cougar capital of Canada, and Kathy Brown's has the reputation of being the cougar capital of London's bar scene. But you won't find just older women here; you're also likely to see a younger group celebrating a birthday or bachelorette party.

The 40-foot-long bar serves up wine, cocktails, and beer – bottled only; there are no draft taps here. There is a good food menu, supplied by the Honest Lawyer's kitchen, which is just down the stairs.

With a $5 cover charge, the door does a brisk business. Staff tells us part of the draw is that, with a capacity of 900, there is never a lineup. This makes it a particularly popular spot on big party nights like St. Patrick's Day and Halloween.

LAVISH
NIGHT CLUB

ELEVATE
ABOVE LAVISH

LAVISH

Built approximately 1884, this deep, narrow space first served as a fancy goods and dry goods store. Today it can again be described as fancy, but certainly not dry. The club features a long list of martinis, cocktails and tropical drinks with catchy and clever names. You can also enjoy a liqueur, wine or beer. The house draft, Cyndi Lager (named for singer Cyndi Lauper) is made for Lavish by a Toronto micro-brewery.

Owner Eddy Phimphrachanh opened Lavish in 2008 as a place "for anyone who wants to feel comfortable being themselves." The club is a popular destination for lesbian, gay, bisexual, transgendered, queer and two-spirited as well as heterosexual individuals who enjoy the upscale dance club atmosphere and, in warm weather, the rooftop patio Elevate.

The historic feel is captured in exposed brick walls and distressed wood floors, but juxtaposed with modern industrial features like exposed ceiling ducts, LED lighting, and a concrete dance floor with dance platforms. The multi-purpose stages are also used for drag shows, Pride events, fashion shows and other occasional live entertainment.

Another of Eddy's unique design features is the open communal sink area between the men's and women's bathrooms. "I wanted to further blur the gender lines, and it's also another area where people can meet and mingle," he says.

The music changes nightly, with top 40 remix on weekends, lollypop retro, electronic house, hip hop and urban music other nights. There is no set schedule and everyone is welcome.

The Scots Corner

London's home for live soccer.

The Scots Corner ⑭
268 Dundas Street

From the time it was built in the 1880s until 1928 the main floor of this building was occupied by a succession of druggists. For a few years the upper floors were operated as a hotel and later as a boarding house.

The space was taken over by the Bank of Montreal from 1935 to 1945, then converted to a restaurant, and eventually to the pub that has operated here for more than 25 years.

The current owner, a genuine Glaswegian, opened the Scots Corner in 1988. There is a huge Robbie Burns Day celebration here each year, and visitors from Scotland find their way to the pub year-round to have a pint and eat authentic haggis and steak and kidney pie. There are 33 beers on tap, the majority British imports.

The pub bills itself as London's home for live soccer and the city's official headquarters for Manchester United Supporters. Soccer fans will come in as early as 7:30 a.m. to watch the games in real time.

The décor is typical British pub, from the framed artwork to the dart board. The walls sport autographed jerseys and brewers' signs as well as a huge graphic of the Glasgow pub crawl. There is an iconic red phone booth just inside the front entrance.

Live music has been a staple since the Scots Corner opened, with entertainment every weekend including a local Irish band. The pub has hosted a weekly open stage since 1996 and karaoke Sundays for more than 20 years.

Repurposed Residential

London's earliest houses were frame structures. There were no purely residential neighbourhoods in the original settlement. Houses, factories, livery stables, banks, the market, hotels, taverns, retailers, churches, the newspaper press and other businesses co-existed in a relatively small area. In 1850, after a series of fires razed large swaths of the village, particularly the great fire of 1845, London passed a by-law prohibiting the construction of wooden buildings within the town's commercial centre.

From that point up to 1914 most houses were clad with locally produced brick, made from clay deposits found in the ground near the Thames River. Five of those historic yellow brick homes are now functioning as pubs.

Each of the five has been described as a "local"– a place that people who live and work nearby regard as a second home of sorts. Locals are socially inclusive places where you can enjoy good food and drink, get to know the regulars, have great conversations, or simply sit and relax. Researcher Theodore Graves, observing the social connections people made over drinks, concluded, "It is the conviviality, not the alcohol, which is of central importance."

*City directories give us a glimpse
into past occupants of the five pubs.*

Mr. William Y. Brunton was the original resident in both the **Black Shire** (1884) and the **Morrissey House** (1889). He was an auctioneer, owner of a dry goods store, and one of the key early organizers of the Western Fair Association. Coincidentally, both houses were later used as offices before being converted to pubs in 2005.

The **Coates of Arms** was built by the Wightons in the mid-1860s and has stayed in the family to this day. As a rental property, it has been home to a seed and dairy supplier, Superintendent of Parks for the City, salesmen, a grocer, a lithographer and other residents, and later to a number of restaurants and pubs.

The **London Music Club** was home to a widow, Mrs. George Harris, and stayed in her family from the early 1880s to the early 1950s when it became the Knights of Columbus hall. Pete and Jan Denomme purchased it in 2004, and it's been filled with music ever since.

The **Runt Club** seems to have been built as a duplex in 1886. The main floor was home to various members of the Tierney family. A variety of tenants have lived upstairs, including a cigar maker, a barber and a Free Press employee.

All five repurposed residential buildings have a welcoming, friendly atmosphere. Perhaps the families that lived in them infused their homes with a warmth that makes people feel instantly at ease.

Fun Fact:

Commissioners Road was once called Brick Street. Several farmers along the road moulded and fired clay from their fields to create the buff coloured brick that graces many of London's historic buildings.

⑮ Black Shire

511 Talbot Street

The original occupant, Mr. William Y. Brunton, was a man of many interests. As well as being a busy entrepreneur, the 1884 City Directory lists "Baptist Church" beside his name. We've been told the house was built as a manse for the First Baptist Church next door, which had been erected in 1882.

The Black Shire has been here since 2010, and every effort has been made to create the atmosphere of an authentic British pub, from the design of the patio to the 17 taps at the bar.

Live music is an important part of the Black Shire's culture. There is a small performance area on the main floor and a large stage upstairs which is regularly booked by local or touring bands.

The Coates of Arms opened in 2010 and is named for Jonathon and Rob Coates, the cousins who own it. With its original wood features and ornate fireplaces in the principal room, the building retains the feel of a Victorian home.

There is live acoustic music weekly, and Scotch or beer tastings monthly. Tasters will often vote to determine the next draft to be carried in the rotating taps. The pub is known by aficionados for its impressive selection of single malt Scotch, boutique wines and premium imported beers.

A former occupant extended the main floor space by adding an atrium. The Coates have since covered the glass walls to create a cozy space that fits with their motto: "Be Warm, Be Welcome, Be at Home."

⑰ London Music Club

470 Colborne Street

This grand old home is full of character, from the coziness of the front parlour to the ornate front staircase that runs right up to the attic. Owners Pete and Jan Denomme opened the London Music Club here in 2004 as a place where people can share their love and appreciation of music.

Pete grew up two doors down, number 12 of 17 children. He remembers having a drink here when it was the Knights of Columbus hall, and family Christmas parties held here when, with the addition of spouses and children, the annual celebration outgrew the family home.

Now the old home hosts more than 400 live performances each year, mainly folk, roots, blues and some rock, in three separate music areas. Enjoy weekly electric jam and acoustic open mic nights, and the monthly London Irish Folk Club ceilidh, London Poetry Slam and comedy improv nights.

This is a home where the musical community connects, and where many friendships and bands have been born.

the power
of music

transform
celebrate
express life

Morrissey House ⑱

359-361 Dundas Street

When owner Mark Serré opened The Morrissey House in 2009, his vision was to create a true "local" like the ones he enjoyed during a stint living in Australia. Regulars will tell you he has created just that, with trivia nights, a fine selection of craft beers, a menu with good food made from scratch, and a comfortable front patio to enjoy in season.

Except for the removal of the original staircase to create more space inside the front doors, the main floor of this old home has been fairly well preserved. There are high ceilings, stretches of exposed brick on the walls and still functioning pocket doors leading into the former parlour. Rumour has it there are even a few resident ghosts hanging about.

⑲ Runt Club

155 Albert Street

This pub, on a side street off Richmond, is in a lovely former residential block. London-born entrepreneur Mike Smith opened the Runt Club in 1990; he also owns Fellini Koolini's Italian restaurant next door. The two share a kitchen, so good food is part of what people expect when they come here.

This was not a large house, and the pub area is quite cozy. Maps on the walls often take people off on conversational topics that span the globe. In warm weather most patrons will sit outside, enjoying shade from a tree that was planted among the tables years ago. It's one thing that makes this pub's patio unique and adds to the Runt Club's relaxing atmosphere.

Cheers!

Cheryl and I have been friends for more than a decade. Neither of us can tell you exactly when we firmed up the concept of Bar Hopping Into History as a book. It seemed like a good idea at the time.

We agreed that Cheryl would create the drawings, I would write the text, and through our words and pictures we would try to share our love of London's historic downtown. We agreed that above all we would have fun with it.

Neither of us is originally from London. Cheryl was raised on a farm in Southwestern Ontario, and I grew up in Northern Ontario. We each remember just how overwhelmed we felt when we first landed in London, ready to take on the big city!

I came to attend Western, and I still remember being struck by the beauty of the campus. After graduation I traveled through Europe. One of my fellow travelers, a recent architect grad, was so enthusiastic about the architectural features in each country that we visited, it was infectious. While I have always been fascinated with stories and sites that are rooted in history, that trip gave me a new appreciation for the aesthetic beauty of London's older architecture.

Cheryl's fascination with historic architecture started in 2007 with a plein air drawing of a Limoux, France streetscape. After traveling in France she started to take notice of the architecture right here in London. Her 2012 show, 'A Homage to London's Downtown', featured renderings of historic London buildings. A recent series entitled 'Tavern Tour' is a continuation of that Streetscapes Series. It concentrates on local taverns and explores the history, culture and spirit of local watering holes.

We have had a lot of fun bringing this project from inception to print. We hope you have enjoyed barhopping into London's history with us.

We would love to hear your feedback on our blog at http://barhoppingintohistory.blogspot.ca.

Cheers, Kym & Cheryl

Bibliography

20CENTSMusic. http://20centsmusic.com/NSB_info.htm.

Aziz, Victor (photo credit). Vintage London, Ontario. 1950s. <https://www.facebook.com/photo.php?fbid=374115269381443&set=a.25912320754731 7.61836.256233541169617&type=1&theater>.

Baker, Michael (Editor). Downtown London Layers of Time. London, ON: The City of London & London Regional Art and Historical Museums, 2000.

Barber, Gina. London Civic Watch. 27 May 2013. <http://ginabarber. blogspot.ca/2013/05/the-hydro-shop-1912-56.html>.

Bell, Del. "York's Frenchy still one of the fastest and best on the draft beer circuit." London Free Press 24 July 1970.

Chinn, Kendra. Londons Legend. Lawson Literary Award project. London, ON, 2008.

City of London. "City Directory." London, ON, 1884-1948.

Cunningham, Violet M. London in the Bush 1826-1976. London, ON: London Historical Museums/London Public Library Board, 1976.

Curnoe, W.Glen. Around London 1900-1950: A Picture History. London, ON: W.Glen Curnoe, 1973.

Evens, J. Michael. Core Heritage: A Survey of Built Heritage In Downtown London Ontario. London ON, 2009.

George, L. and Barry Wells. Alt London. 2013 <http://www.altlondon. org/article.php?story=20090901180023187>.

"Insurance Plan of the City of London, Ontario, Canada." Montreal: Charles E. Goad Co., Surveyed October 1881 revised July 1888.

"Insurance Plan of the City of London, Ontario, Canada." Montreal; Toronto; London, Eng.: Charles E. Goad Co., Surveyed February 1892, revised July 1907.

"Insurance Plan of the City of London, Ontario, Canada." Montreal; Toronto; Winnipeg; London, Eng.: Charles E. Goad Co., Surveyed February 1912 revised March 1915.

"Insurance Plan of the City of London, Ontario, Canada." Toronto; Montreal: Underwriters Survey Bureau, Surveyed February 1892, revised and reprinted February 1912. Revised April 1922.

"Historic Plaque." London Hydro Shop, 1912 to 1956. London ON: London Public Library Board and London Hydro Inc., 2013.

"Historic Plaques." 122 Carling Street, The Farmer's Advocate. London, ON: London Public Library Board, 1990, 2011.

Johnson, Erin. The History of 216 York Street, London Ontario. Essay for LIS 9326, Western University. London, ON, 2012.

Johnston, Wayne A. At The York. London, ON: Ergo Productions, 1990.

London Ontario. London, ON: The London Printing & Lithographic Company, Limited, 1914.

London Public Library Board. Walking Guide to Historic Sites in London. London, ON: Historic Sites Committee of the London Public Library Board, 2005.

London, Tourism. Tourism London. 2013 <http://m.londontourism.ca/ Places-To-Eat/Barneys-Lounge-and-Bar---The-Ceeps>.

McTaggart, Ken. London's Darkest Hours. London, ON: Ken D McTaggart, 1999.

Miller, Orlo. London 200: An Illustrated History. London, ON: London Chamber of Commerce, 1992.

Miller, Orlo. This Was London: The First Two Centuries. Westport, ON: Butternut Press Inc., 1988.

Mullin, Mary. Life in Victorian-Edwardian London Ontario 1867-1914. Essay, History 362, University of Western Ontario. London ON, 1974.

"Sansone Fruit closes doors, site up for sale." London Free Press 31 March 1972.

Smith, George L. A History of London in Pictures. Bright's Grove, ON, 1971.

Social Issues Research Centre. The Enduring Appeal of the Local. <http://www.sirc.org/publik/the_local.shtml>.

St-Denis, Guy (Editor). Simcoe's Choice: Celebrating London's Bicentennial 1793-1993. Toronto, ON: Dundurn Press Limited, 1992.

Tausky, Nancy Z. Historical Sketches of London from Site to City. Peterborough, ON: Broadview Press, 1993.

The London Printing & Lithographing Company (Limited), Designers and Engravers. City of London Ontario, Canada. The Pioneer Period and The London of Today. London, ON: The London Printing & Lithographing Company (Limited), Designers and Engravers, 1900.

The W.T. Rawleigh Company. <http://www.rawleigh.net/Rawleigh_History.htm>.

www.ingramcontent.com/pod-product-compliance
Lightning Source LLC
LaVergne TN
LVHW010025070426

835509LV00001B/16